THE LAUNDRYMAN'S GRANDDAUGHTER

The Laundryman's Granddaughter
POEMS

Arlene Kramer Richards

International Psychoanalytic Books (IPBooks)
New York • http://www.IPBooks.net

THE LAUNDRYMAN'S GRANDDAUGHTER POEMS

Published by IPBooks, Queens, NY
Online at: www.IPBooks.net

ISBN: 978-1-956864-18-2

Contents

CONTENTS

The Laundryman's Granddaughter

Ride me in your pushcart.
A bump from rough canvas white sacks of dry; towels, socks,
    washcloths and knit underwear:
To sacks frozen concrete-grey by wet wash;
blouses, ruffled and plain; slips edged in eyelet, laced with pale blue
    satin ribbons, skirts pleated across
the front, table napkins and pillowcases.
and back to soft white sacks, made grateful by ice-wet sharpness
    entering flesh.
I roll from brown paper crackling oblongs of flat: shirts, sheets,
    tablecloths.
I love me here.
You stop. Terror. A bundle of wet wash. Don't
Leave me.
Carry me up dizzy bumps of stairs.
Let me ride balance to your bundle
Innards jiggle, gaggly as cream soda.
I want man-hard warm shoulders under me.
Carry me. Carry me. Never put me down.
Until I Grab the knife from your belt. Slash our rope,
never is not so long, and open the bundle of myself.

Brighton Laundry

Sheets 9 o'clock, pillowcases 12,
shirts 3, tablecloth 6,
all the flatwork round the clock
builds a timescape on a raw floor.

Mrs. Goldberg has a mountain of flat this week. Grandfather
   Laundryman and I sort her mountain
into four orderly hills. You and I.

My playground is here in your laundry.
You let me do the 7:30 napkins myself.
I plane wetwash, clock center,
into a black-green sliced-off mesa
with my toes. I skate on
socks, shorts, undershirts
in the middle of time's kingdom.
Banished to the corner, dry stands of towels,
eyelet-edged teddies and pale buckets of handkerchiefs wait for
   sorting.
Twenty years later, the son stands on my pale wool carpeting,
asking to come into my sorting room.
I measure him out a comfortable chair.
He sits in the gold corduroy chair.
He, magician, pulls stacks of linen
from his sleeves.
I wonder at the colors.
He starts to make a mountain.

I help sort out.
Some belong to table, some to bed.

He calls himself shocked at the smells,
eyes me to see if I gag,
smiles back at my chin.
I sit simple here.
He pulls out sheets stained with piss.
Damp wash, I say. Damp goes to the middle.
We dance on the piles under the moon.
Whirling on shrouds, we pout on the soap.
Bubbles splash, tickling our nipples, the milk comes. Around, the
    long minute hand sweeps past,
closes a circle,
leaving others.
We'll go around again.
Giddly with dancing, flushed peach with moving,
we bow, shake hands and part,
We'll collect again next week.
We pick up Monday.

Retired

Your eyes went first. They pell-melled down to shut out cries and
Gabriel Heatter on the radio.

Your eyes blurred away dreams dolls and pictures of your thirteen
busy brothers and sisters.

Your skin grew thick. It piled up horn like young antelope's head
bones to butt packing case ropes.

Your taste buds shriveled against the garlic pepper mixed pickling
spice and oily matjes herring.

Your smell grew with not touching your own skin, not washing, until it
shut out all other smells.

All your senses had retired before you did. You were retired in Poland
father, in New York father, in Fort Lauderdale father.

Sorry

I must hop out after loving
Leaving your bed-warming back, Bruising your masculine
Pride by moving now.
Don't lemon juice
Acid shock that I
Sing.
Navel
Orange,
nectarine sterile,
I pay with delight in orders of words. Blake
knew better, Anne Frank
worse than Texas grapefruit.
We do not die.

Secretarial Help

Morning:
I sit in the next room,
trembling to the charge
of your uncompleted morning love,
The one your wife left over.
I shiver slightly at my desk,
imagining you'll call through
rubber walls and let me
know when to
come to you.

Noon:
On 46th Street, small dark men
with square heads
sharpen their eyes,
honing them along
along the strop of my body
    until, razor keen, they cut
through my coat, shirt, pangs, and
leave me cantering
naked down 45th Street

Evening:
I stop to buy mums for
a centerpiece,
maybe you'll come for dinner.
And a coffeecake,

Maybe you won't
I hold the green paper cone
of sun-shined mums
      on top of the cream cardboard cube reeking with butter.

Blind fingers search
the Africa dark interior
of my well-tanned leather bag
      for keys.
Finder's losers,
empty keepers.
I make the seconds last.
As long as I don't go in,
I won't know what
and if you left your say
on my machine.

Post Office

I walk my loneliness, my excuse for a dog, to the post office.
I turn back.
I will not mail the letter.
I will not know you gone.

Bag Lady

Beige smiling,
skinny woman
carries three shopping bags through the checkout aisle at the
   supermarket.
I see her past window,
under glass.
She eats half her bag of cookies.
The man at the register points to the bag.
   I think he wants to charge her less—
The bag is half empty.
Or maybe give her a new bag—
that one is only half-full.
She shakes her refusal,
sweeps change
over the silvery counter,
birdwings her fingers
over the bags
under her eyes.

Promised Land

A broad highway; road interior,
hacked gently up that piny hill
to my wilderness,
so I can walk in pleasantness
through cedar forests
of denial, where,
only years ago,
the going required risk of life and shank. Over my song of thanks,
   even lightening thunder
Aaron's golden calf, fatted on bluepoint oysters,
sing, he is still as Moses,
who, by halting, reining in his speech,
allowed, partly by what was missing,
me and all to fight open.

Deer Isle

Dawn exposes pink underbellies of western clouds,
I sit alone, awake, only the birds and I
know this day's smoothness.
Creamy sunshine moves the still calm Penobscot waters of the bay.
I walk our small land.
Evening primrose grins yellow in the still gentle-enough light
Asters spring back as I pass, Berries offer sweetness.
My love still sleeps.
I dare not wake him.
He sleeps.

Moving Day

Alone in my appraisal,
solitary under black trees,
I set edged at any sorrow,
Proud I cleared barriers of morning purple fallen leaves
away and away.

I scraped soft from roots and rocks,
Past berm, to outcropping
Bedrock under the soft sheet.
To my lonely bedpost freedom,
Licensed, even, to sell my own real estate
To when and whom
I will. To please.

Concert, January 30, 1975

He trembled.
His bronze face shone behind
his strings,
burning pupils into my eyes.

His lips opened.
I saw his tongue
nursing nursling infant effort from
the roof of his mouth to fingers,
    slashing light from his strings.
Zabaleta, magic harpist, trembled,
made an error, stopped, announced it, began Da Capo

And, and, shot Spanish black
like missiles, targeted to hope-reddened
young musicians in the first row
to worship the master's fingers.

a road to the top of the property.

Acoustic Neuroma

He unwinds the ball of nerve string
from out her left ear,
pulling opera, concerts,
Traffic, quarrels, strung bead
lovely, stuck in the order they came in.
She hears the nerve wine as it
dies after the operation.
Slowly, month by minute;
minute by month.

He took the R.R. center in his
Ether-green robe. Slipped
it out of the tip of the scalpel,
pulling gentle, getting it
from the middle,
leaving a hollow shell.
He was filming all the while.
For teaching purposes.

The intensive care recovery room
was where she called him
wait, I need to know who will teach me purpose?

He came, straining her words,
winding them still on,
winding them still on his growing balls.
His string collection.

She watched her own surgeon grow.
Joined now, lined to each other.
She whispered. Teach me to spin.
Violin back my sounds.

Aaron

Simple golden-rod, unfairly maligned,
raised golden sex away from green,
Aching toward pale blue wash sky.
In England, they call it Aaron's Rod.
Fertile Aaron thrives in drought,
makes quiet miracles under Moses' arm.
You freshen my spring in a dry search.
I love, why my Aaron and the sky,
simple, no hubris, best.

You are my warm day, lean-on,
my stand-tall man. I love you
as I loved the mother struck with hay fever.
For her sake, we trained to New Hampshire
Forever white mountain woods where golden-rod
never grows. Thanks, I thanked her. Thanks
Filled with raspberries, stuffed with sunlight,
Cooled with night dew,
I waited content for golden-rod days
and you.

Egyptian Collection

Bast: An Egyptian Goddess of War and Physicians

Bast of the white face,
Bast of the lion head,
goddess of fire, tail, leaping
goddess of ware, toothed, sighing,
the yellow card tells me who you are.
You are the goddess of physicians,
Sister, I too consort with semites
I wear a shadow of the yellow star.

I know what it is to be tall, toothed,
and worshiped.
I wish onto your forever night,
you are into my days.
We sigh together,
I for night, you for days.
We keep together the secret hollow
for worshipers
who want to touch
you in me,
me in you.

Sauna

Four bodies overlapped as wooden benches
Three women envy
one who looks endless,
a forever of limbs, breasts, disappearing into her nipples, as she lies
    on her back, hipbones jutting at steep angles, round only at the
    curve of her ribs
where they stretch the skin of her chest,
recognizing the self in that body brave enough to let
the skeleton show, content with the thinnest envelope
around her death;

One whose fat billows as venous foam bubbling out
of sand-pale skin, opalescent clam whiteness, her
oyster-blue face, whose days are elongated in pleasure; herb omelets,
    exquisite cakes, perfumes, potpourri, dried flowers,
conversation hearts, ice creams, her breath rippling the fat waist ring
    that marries her to death;

One who lisps of a lawyer son as she after-shave smooths her thighs
    with grass-scented cream, as she greens her day with bearing
    generations, printed-tissue-wrapped beautiful fruits in concert
    salad,
wrapping away her own days,

enduring again and yet the longest fretful sleepless nights of waiting
    for them to grow order, waiting for them to grow older, waiting
    until she knows only

how to wait until the rings under her eyes are slipped
onto the finger of death;
one who pulls herself out over red continents and black
oceans
between he and me and she and me, and overhears all
the secrets they want her to hear and know and hear
so they don't have to listen to them alone, and hugs her secrets
to her heavy breasts, knowing all day long
that the smell of them witches men to vampires,
to nurse on her blood all night.

Four women here, set in wood, becoming stone
lasting as bikini-bathers set in mosaic at Piazza Armorina,
summer home of Roman emperors and the leavings of Crusaders:
the blue-eyed, the cross-eyed, French-speaking Sicilian brat.
They set life on benches, overlapped in envy, set in stone.

Doctor A

You do not wish to know of gorillas,
Blood-red wounds bursting into flame, Explosions of torn flesh don't
   move you
    so much as academic professions
Cherry-name inherent observations.
What tidbit of genius can I serve you today,
Sir?
The slow moving coils of my feet,
a winter-torpid snake
Coil about your neck,
Enveloping you in velvety woman-softness
Eve imagined you seduced, grizzled, ridiculous; weeps.

Pour on the balm of Gilead
Refresh me with the taste of joy.
Fountain waters sparkle cleanly.
Do not settle here for less.
Compromising with the victor jumps into the boiling foam,
keeps us far from Grandma's cauldron.
sends us, dressed now, far from home.

Dying

My vegetarian Buddhist friend sat in the delicatessen.
There's nothing left, she said, but cancer and inflation. From my
    teacup, shards of glassy light danced
tears onto my palms.
I held your crystal neck so hard, enough.
I loved your edges close, enough.
I made you the man who pulls brilliant tomorrows
from the leaves. Lean shards in the fat droplets, ice spines, collided
    my back to the wall. You didn't want me.

At home that afternoon,
dying in a mirror,
watching my reflection,
winking at it,
drawing blood to the meat beating sparkle of applause
    I arched my back, and back.

After the Hospital

You wanted out.
Your hand filled its grease-spotted brown paper of skin
to bursting
Blue cord veins in sailor's knots held the package together,
Farther up your arm, plastic pipes bound you
to the bottles over your white-barred prison.
You kicked as they forced tubes at your nose, down your throat,
by passing your tongue and self.
Your keg-bellied Arab of a surgeon filled your chest with nylon
    arteries, looped.
He thought he could put the cage inside you. He wanted to tie you to
    life. For good.

You fought back.
Even the night you walked, mended at last,
up the narrow tin-roofed hallway,
to meet the killer
as he drove
switchblade and death
between your bonecage ribs.
Over-tired; that's what he must have been.
Blue devils flew baroque ovals round his thigh.
Theater friends knew fantasy, light as
Pop-overs, nourished plump his scientific calm.
He jumped. Teasing God. He couldn't fly.
Loving man; desired; manning love.
Hedged unpleasing bets gentling home.

Popov confined for deviationist dissent.

The eater. Fried ends of newspaper-cone fish and chips disgusted
him.

Blue devils astride his drawn-down sword.

Overt ire at least, he couldn't wait for; spring.

Tell Me

Out with it. Why let all that good stuff rattle around in your head?
Circulating through reverberating circuits?
Keep it coming. The foolish along with the pointedly Accurate.
There, that man sitting beside me on the bus. Old.
He fastens his folded newspaper to his several times re-folded brown
   paper bag
With three bronze paper clips.
Having reorganized the books, I'm ready for a girl-scout rescue
   mission.
Get any Halloween-headed kids around?
I'm ready for a fright.

Mer

At 3:30 my nightmare rides me out of bed.
Red blotches flatter black way.
A year-long swamp festers in the salt water tank
my husband neglects to prove/deny his manliness.
I eat all night, agreeing with him that my sleeplessness is
    physiological
When I reach 3:30, he will divorce me

Oysters can't be hurried, he says.
The longer they live, the bigger they grow, I say.
Your pearl will come, he says.
But not me, I say.
My nightmare is a seahorse, she cannot gallop on land.
It is my night, the sea.

Only the shore is dangerous.
Fish and I drown at the border.

Halloween

Your ghost ate chocolates and refused to ski.
Mine drank music and wore boots.
Yours loved to shop, to throw furious pots. Mine finally removed his
  red toupee.

Our ghosts dance on the shaggy green rug,
between us.
We'll fold their sheets, to and bottom,
to make our bed.

David's Widow

Sitting alone in my apartment,
I swell with aloneness
As I recall your days.
Now you are not tell,
Not empowered or disciplined.
Not on your harp, not effulgent.
Now here is:
No column; no sounding board; no strings;
Quiet at last, as I've always wanted it.
Silence shrieks you
gone and gone.
I remember complaining then. You never
spoke my name.
Now your chair accuses me,
tells me, among the words you never said
were no and won't and can't;
sends me to the door, to call
Out.

Saturday Sunday

Silky on tongue as melting icecubes or instant
oatmeal;
Moustache sweet under the arched palate.
Maroons glacés, Those chocolate covered marshmallows adorned
    with garment-manufacturing Jewish names
and oversimplified Stars of David melt. The present pluperfect
Accompaniment to Leonard Bernstein's Mass,
Performed in full sunlight to excruciated
knots of floor-sitting Westside longchairs
Burgeon warmth through that facial flesh
one adorns to give pleasure and is shocked to find
exploding blushes of delight inward toward the brain.

The Husband

A long woman green as pale trees
Stands in my doorway
Going in or coming out
She waits there as if
For a signal
To push her

One way or
The other.
Poised between she sways
And I wonder
Can she stop
Over a threshold?
She goes
I come Apart.

Sweetback Man

Bubbles of me splurting up
To your headylips, nethertongue.
Slashwise greening riplets up nylons,
Congressional festoons countersplish acrosticwise.
Settle New England fall under a tree.
Simpleballs snowflake under my hat.
Youngerly, youngerly, merryman Joan.
Come standupnow, standupnow, whethergreen corn.
Everpale underwood leaflet green sky.
Overmy, overmy booby pink eyes.
Tattooflies nammywise nightorn green cloud.
Rianose puoronme, slinky dingle dangle.
Voiceover singunder swingalong man.
Ready. Set. Come.

Lushful temptalong moonbeamy dates.
Palmtickle lightnights uppersong fates.
Dibbubles foamingup standard green raised.
And down and down in the neverplace.

Never is over. My finger's unpricked.
Yourself woke me up.

I want to be your shoesandsox.

Prize in your crackerjackbox.

Whiffle in shiverbrees. Riffles in pepperbush.
Sing in me echohall.
Play me your lollyfruit. I want to sleep home.

Oh Daddyme diddleman
Ready. Set. Come.

Songings in passiovow
Ripple me shiverknees.
Quiddle me elbowing.
Move me up spindleshin. Dindle me. Dandleme.
Shoot me through space.
Wandleme, downdonme,
I'll play your flute.
Flutleme, toolme,
Eachtoeach singing.
Ready. Set. Come.

Letter to Someone Who Said it Was Necessary

The year I was eight, my cousins went to the stadium outside Paris,
    France; I was at Ebbets Field, outside New York, America.
I saw the Dodgers.
They got transport: Drancy to Auschwitz.
Train wheels pound the rhythm. Bound. Bound.
The red of their blood sings in my dreams.
America. America.

Years later in a stadium outside Santiago
Reds stood waiting for quicker transport.
But first blue sport. First Victor Jara.
The white hands of Victor Jara.
    reach out to me across the band of years.
Alone, without their arms, they reach.
At night they reach America. I put them to bed
    on my pillow. Now they live in America.
Some nights they play the guitar as they used to before they were
    sacrificed.
He sang his hope when they accompanied him He sang defiance
    after they were hacked off.
He sang while his time ran out with the blood from his wrists.
He sings to me still, and still.

Florine Stettheimer—Self Portrait

Languid,
pale,
alone,
on a narrow bed,
fish hipped,
slim as a barracuda,
her feet curved upward
in a tail.
This object of satin desire
Subjects us with
paint on cheek
as on easel-bedded canvas.
Her sheets to the wind,
She could not
care less.

Itta and Lycha

Itta was born in Chechanow, Poland. Because her family was very
poor, she was sent
to live with her Aunt and Uncle and their daughter Lycha in their very
comfortable
Warsaw house. Lycha's mother had been unable to have other
children, so Itta was a
companion for her daughter. The
girls loved to ice-skate until one day Lycha taunted Itta
about not being the real
daughter of the family and therefore having to do
whatever Lycha wanted or she would
be sent back to her poor village. Itta took offense, and
kicked Lycha, causing a
compound fracture that never healed properly. As a result, Lycha was
crippled, never
left her parents' home and died in the Holocaust. Itta kept a secret
picture of them
together where her children could never see it.

I know now why eggs are eaten on arriving home from the cemetery.
I see now the dirt I need to shovel in.
I stand beside the grave she made her bed, looking down into her
private hell as she sees Lycha
the dead cousin, dark beauty of the concentration camp.

Once they were girls skating together on an ice lake near Warsaw,
quarrelling as girls will when one has the parents,

the other, no orphan but taken in, lives as her companion.

Lycha teases Itta, pulls her hair.

They tumble in a ball of wool and flash of blade.

Ice trees shake, shattering silver needles from the twigs.

Their world freezes over.

Lycha, the darling only girl stares at her cracked leg. Itta screams and
  skates for home and help.

Swoops back to Lycha, trailing grownups in her wake.

They carry home the broken girl.

The cripple who will never marry,

ready for the oven.

Out of the shell, my mother is born.

Fearful, strong, fearful, weak, determined, fearful

she knows she belongs to the weak.

She wants to find the evil.

She meets my father, sees in him a stronger shell, |
  but just as easily cracked. Just as easily cracked.

And has the babies Lycha will never.

And fearful overfeeds, fearful wraps in warm wool,

Fearful keeps indoors, fearful falls and bleeds and loses her baby,

Fearful blames me her darling only daughter, her Lycha, her demon,
  her avenger.

Lycha calls me. How can I avenge a crime I do not know?

Avenge. Destroy.

I run from that work.

She finds a daughter-in-law with the stomach for it.

Daintily, her tiny mouth pursed,

her long silver icepick poised,

she strikes and cracks the shell that was my mother.

My Mother

A black stain oval on the earth,
she stands on the scorch mark
destroying angels,
destroying devils,
She has a simple policy, stand in the burn
untouched as morning ironing
left while the coffee boils over on the stove,
while the children cry, while ice boxes drip.
She swoops elegantly through the scald,
dancing with mah jong tiles swinging in her ear.
look at my dress, my dress, my own self, look at me standing and
    bowing and scraping
a violin melody from the radio.
Look at me, look at me, look at me now.

Mad Hatter's Tea Party

Table's set in a hurry:
white lace cloth, blue napkins
Here's Uncle Irving
Sitting at the table.
Slap him on the head
With a yellow saucer.
Here's Aunt Gracie
standing by his chair.
Slap her on the beak
with a pink teacup.
Tweak Aunt Sylvia's
peachy ear.
Pull her head beneath her knees.
Don't bother Morris,
Dead child-beater.
Pauline's head gets pushed down,
pleats into her neck.
Goodbye you nasty beasties
Good buy envious elders.
Worth it, every penny.
Good bye and bye and bye.

The Paintings

Renoir—*Dancing at the Moulin de la Galette*
We are in love, center left. You
are wearing top hat, I'm in white.
How close your arms pull me, your hands on my ass. You're drunk
   and telling outrageous things and kissing my ear.
Why did you always say you couldn't dance?
Isn't it grand in the sun?
 I have nothing on under my white dress.
I can feel your erection, perfectly.

Boudin—*Lunch in A Garden*
Not the couple in the foreground,
but seated behind red roses
nearly under the trees, talking
intently. So seriously. Philosophy,
I think, Why is the man, brown hat
in his hand, looking at us? I'll have more wine. Lunch in a garden,
Two glasses of wine and I'll say,
I love you.

Renoir—*The Breakfast of the Boating Party*
Upper right corner, you in black derby.
We're arguing. God knows we 're not dressed
for boating, like the others, You had to
cover the story and told me to meet you,
Don't give me that shit about poets escaping
pain and ugliness of everyday life, while

Journalists know reality. It's arrogant
of you to suffer. See the man
in the red cap who's listening to me.
He says the lady's right, He says
everybody here could tell you plenty
about trouble, He says that doesn't mean
it isn't a glorious day for a boating party.

Morning in Palm Beach When Sunrise Brings Color to the Crows' Feathers.

Apron-clad Latina
scuttles through South Ocean Drive; black
crows strut across, sun greens.

Meeting Winnie, The Poodle

Friendly? Yes but you
have to be careful.
He's a serial kisser.

Before Dawn

Mutton-fat clouds press
Indigo sky; hide moon that
illuminates them.

Look, Sun coming up.
Day. Squirrling into brain
through optic nerves. Wake.

Foam clouds hide rising
sun. Overhead blue fades to ice
at horizon's edge.

February 12, 2019

Fulminating cloud
spirals up from Southeast, rages,
floats, no danger now.

Ominous red streak
Morning Eastern sky
Will I get home dry?

Ending

Sleep me up a dream,
I told my solo self.
Fill my cup to overflowering,
slip me in an ivory knife.

Standing between dawn and morning,
erecting his usual wall, he is
turning his shoulder so my face
meets his backbone, my arms his
elbowing arms
presenting his heels to my
exploring thighs, he
runs from me in his sleep.

Father

You were the wine of my enchantment,
Giving me heart to pump the day's reality
Through the grey-sponge mountains and out the
Sylvan fissure.

Your white nights
Out in the Russian field with stars and farmboys
Fed your courage
Through the everlasting push, mostly unsuccessful,
To bring over fathers and brothers you'd left there.
They sustained me, too.

Once, my green son wanted to bike cross-country,
Visit Oregon, see the Pacific
Powered only by his longing thighs.
Caution, wise friend warned me, caution and care.
Let him go by bus, take a ten-age camping caravan
With leaders and chaperones.

Only your wine-white nights fed me
Hope and trust and carelessness.
I blessed his trip and five-thousand miles later
Welcomed first a man who'd seen the ocean.

Now they say you invited murder, black and red.
Carrying your payroll case in hand.
What can I tell them, Father?

45

Untitled

Love, when I stand in your umbra, shaded
from storms,
the gray hope of morning wraps me like a cape.
I am again a rank beginner
Juices flow under rain flow
I am renewed and new again
The moon and I, come Thursday,
Are reborn.

To Paris

Magpie-wise by candlelight, gathering next year's visual sense
from this year's French ladies' magazine,
resisting the temptation to beat the mean.
I need a padded room in an unpadded mentality
to achieve the exquisite infantile gentility of
Couth—
Achieved first and made thereby not inaccessible
So much is unwilling of access by
Proust.
Publicity destroys. Therefore the neurotic
Insistence on
Callousness, protecting tender flesh.
Proud.

To Arnie

Green goings slivered into multiple shards
That stream like cellophane from a translucent dome.
Jellyfish quicksilver, glassy arrows for his not yet.
He gathers them slowly. Not in any
Particular order. As if he didn't, believe
The cruel chains of time would ever bind so deeply into his flesh as to
Cripple the writing hand,
Decimating all those hard-on exterior pathways
Hacked through chaos. But structuring world,
his hand, eye, ear, skin, nose, mind creates it
In a unique version that doesn't last forever,
Hurry back, love, and hold me, hard.

And death must have his dominion.
He must fill the morning spaces with
New wrinkled free smoothness of cheek,
Enlarge his dominion beyond our simple today
By charging the composition of the human group.
Only death can give us time.
Without his period, we'd have no span.
No whole we could divide into units
However much
his bitter-sweet period closes our sentence.
Thus gives it structure; purpose filled the span.
without it lacunae would echo into caverns,
Mocking us, lost explorers, with endless mirrored sounds
Our own voices waving back, cancelling and expanding our
words to shrieks.

The Hen Rejected

In black
is how
you want me
Thin, pale
And mourning
for the
endless
missed and missing
yolks
shimmering
under
my belly
Strong
and in black
plain
feathered black
I slam cartons
on tables
unbutton my blouse
show breasts
display navel
lure you with feed
scatter corn.
You save your flapping
for the other one.

The Garden

The day glare and near the hedge
A bird bath with dead flies

and dull hum. Listen!
Is it the sun spinning? Or bees

Hovering close to the ground?
The earthworms are disturbed.
They hug together and wait.

Television Looney Tunes

A bit less serious or a little more fun.
Whichever.
You've got to keep it light or the weight of fallen
soufflé will get you down
It's a long way from Cousteau's Calypso
Dragging fallen stalagtites formed in the Bahamas
To the DOA cosmonauts and our senator from Alaska
Crying publicly because the country of Jefferson and Madison
Has been sold down the river by a rig of international
Dope-pushers. Incredible juxtapositions like that
Don't happen everyday, do they?
I mean, we all knew Russian technology was super,
Didn't we? And democracy? Something is real, isn't it?

Surprise

I never thought I would write a book of poems.
Cover green-case paper with them.
But notebooks can't be filled with thought only
If anything is.
So I carry just a mail-sized pouch
Hanging between shoulder-tip and collarbone.
Large enough to carry messages from of those
      readers on menus posted outside restaurants
To entice wary and fond alike
Holding the tiny slip-filled questions
For the great rabbi of the semi-circular court.
Like a hollow spoke through which segments of the rim
Transfer bumps in the road pressures, pothole tensions
Put wobbles in your straight thought.
That whistle, arrow, bone clean slash making for, need, flesh
Sweet.

Subway

Readers of the *Wall Street Journal*
whose shoulder blades stick out like breasts, have bony nipples are
   nourished like Miner va
by Stanley's pert ideas. The ones he
gathered painfully from Genet, blindness,
Gide, the dark Soledad, cobwebs, lizards,
closeness to death, bat dung, in short
all sources of supply available to West Siders
looking for frontiers without end,
oily gushers, gold veins, bonanzas,
ice cream cones and the endless feed of Death.

Mother

You slam and slam again
Your gentle curses across my eye.
You stud my jade green fields
With butter and white demands
For endless imitations
of your single set.
You would drain my greed
to downing straw.
You call for grandchildren
as I used to call for lambchops.

In that kitchen covered with oilcloth
Where apple and orange and banana
Leered from their oval plaster plaque,
I sat a thousand Thursdays
As flounder mixed its pale salt smell
With burning butter and twice-baked flour
and waited to grow old enough

You sit far now, reverse the charges,
On the rent end of the wire,
Clicking your caps like castanets,
your only concession to Spanish Florida
Have a girl for me. Let her eat your heart out.
Let her tell you what you told me.
And when she grows, emit my demand.
And pass it on.

Morning

Tides out, moon's gone,
empty. Suns sparks, and flats.
Magenta, black, muddy brown,
Spruce blue, celadon, purple
Emerge, silvered out
Of young brown silt.
I watch, blood and other juices
Concentrating my eyes.
Many-colored bronze morning
flattens, curves up, rises
like my man in the morning.
I flex scalp, neck shoulders
Upper arms, elbows, forearms, wrists, fingers;
I heave shoulders, back, waist,
Belly, Venus mountain,
My toes arch, feet wire complex arcs
To heel, ankle, calf, knee, thigh, sex.
I roll to meet him,
Find fecund colors trembling
Past each earthy flesh,
Moon and tide rise in us.
We fill each other, full.

Mary Ann

A row of parrot bright ribbons across your chest
Shivers me to think of blood on grass-sprinkled earth
And blood on white ship. Indigo crewel thread blue
Makes blood shine, flowering out over the dark woolly surface.
That's okay now. Gonna be all right now.
Blood flows into bubbly pinkness as you suck it up
Into the saline primed syringe. Happy fulsome candy-wrapper purple.
Lightened up with sunshiny candy-wrapper yellow.
Strong lights, sharp nights, black skies,
The mystery guest who is coming to dinner next Tuesday
That pair I'd forgotten by remembering only that they said
They'd come to dinner at 7:30 on July 12
Birdwise, I snatch enamel pseudo-jewels from the ransom
Trinket-case and feather our nest
With pirate-treasured booty.

Lunar Equinox

The Maya drew their water from *cenotes* limestone cisterns. Since
 they were not wells, the *cenotes* held water only when there was
 rain. Chac was their rain God.

Sheer stone cylinder sunk in wine cool earth
my well. I thought,
how lovely to have my own well,

Splashing fireflies, dragonflies, devil's darning needles, New World
 insect eaters played
the width of my well.

Then, like the Mayan cenote, a terrible mouth, hair-fringed teeth,
 slashing jaw pushed forward the elaborated snout, Chac.

Not a well then. A cenote, cistern, a storager
of water. In short, a rainbarrel
remembering a limestone ideal.

Ancient seas formed me. No. I Rm not
as a spring fed continuously from below,
not bloody but thirsty, a woman now.

Now the land is not fertile.
Will you dare the sacrifice,
dive and die?

Plagues

There was that year in Africa
rain enough and pruning
and too much and splashing
until, pouring,
It washed the red sand down
Into the rivers. Earth invaded waters
Fish flicked and sanded death
off their fins. They shied away from dying,
Flittering, marring, moving,
Fish and star-flecked
fish congealed in
Jelly and mounds
Under backs.
Living water consecrated earth
Fascinating leaves pulled anthrax
In their wake.
Moses saw and shivered.
Yahweh had begun.
He came to visit
Under the skirts of his
Old and ever-nurse Death
Time to go tell Aaron
Time to announce the plagues.
They pace red, squared-off

tiles on the
Waiting-room floor

They are tall men.
Each of them wants a piece
With cream and sugar
Of cake.
They need, before all

To fill their mugs
With icicle
Slaps
Their holsters.
The police men
Badge and a peace
Holster and a piece.

Persephone

One September picnic,
A small black god snapped out
From between the willow roots.
He pulled me after him into his night hole.
Sweeping his cape around us.
I was content.

The sun shrieked.
She lumbered around the house.
She wanted her own back.
Her men scrambled to find me.
I bit the green apple to find out.
I did not hold back— even knowing
the belly-ache to come.

Six pits I spit
half a year below.
I grew tall,
Swollen as wheat stalks,
good again for giving bread.
Night renewed
The juice sun had dried.
Cold and damp,
I shivered, content.

Patient

Pay up he says
Renumerate me
In the only coin
I love, know.

Can this be my vocation, to know?
Never to share the knowing
But merely here, unknown to know?
Too funny, too strange
Unfathomable yet,
But not for always. No

Patty cake, patty cake Baker's man
Bake me a cake as fast as you can.
Pat it and bake it and mark it
With B
And put it in the over for Solomon and me.

He, knowing still knows. Noing knows and knowing noos.
His eyes see, icy soft and wet. Not we.
Who can know it? Who dares? You are brave to care.

July, 1971

Like a squared-off spiral, this cornered maze,
As the Germans say, Mit Ecken, has simple door.
One can easily punch the operculum open and come out on the
    other side
Of maternity. Holding a blanket instead of the bag.
Gently stroking side of face, mutton side, duckside;
Served, in place of lamb in Holy Mary Mother of
God,
Adder to the population explosion;
Women of all seasons, true to yourself, at least
Ruined, tortured like those unfortunates persuaded to stage a mock
    revolution
So their government could legitimately knock them off
Before they could plan a real one. Yet faithful somehow,
True as cucumbers. Envy Mary, not because she had God explore
Inside her, but because she had that snaily slow walk
Your own mucus shiny path inside.

Homage to Sappho

You stalk into my room
Wrapped in your cloak of silence
Pulling my eardrums slingshot-taut
Ready to snap at your word.

I fear your gentleness, tender girl
Your quiet cost is steel and your
Soft glance a sword.

What—will you cut these elastic strands
So soon and leave me torn
And bleeding?

Heavy Metals

Air-conditioned subway cars turn metal eye-glass frames
Stretched from nose bridge to outer ear like English country towns
Into icy shackles, chaining me to trykes past
Time demands these turns as meter
Forces ordinary words into poetry,
Pushing reality to the corners of my desk, it
Pulls me out of the computer room
Good wrinkle, simulated leather baseboard automobile,
And into this realer world of fantasy
Sensations hiked to ice-high levels.
Shudder my bonds into clench-tooth subway.
Let the fantasy out of his box like a
Jack out of the pulpit, dur doer door
Adeiu.

He Died who Lives

He was the final edition,
a particular dinosaur,
last of his line.

I never knew what he had perfected
so absolutely
no further revisions were necessary.

He lived, moustache-young, frog easy,
palms open
to let anyone take a handful of his time.
He gave days, smiles, unspare minutes
So freely, anyone
would have thought him fit only for endless shallows.
He spread his own as glad hand on the water.

But after his last day,
I saw sprouting from some deeper pools,
that gallant, careless,
day-and-night smile, borne on wind.

He smiled too young,
We were not ready to greet his death,
So keep his faith
And smile it at each other.

Gentleman Sheepherder

When they hung his bleeding liver, brown-red
Against the pale blue Northern sky,
Dangled from tree limb, dark sharp green
Against the pale blue sky,
The beauty of this day transliterated
Against the pale blue Northern sky
Containers of blood waved gaily as hers
Against the pale blue sky.
Greek tragedy for him, who loved too easily
Against the pale blue Northern sky,
On her white soft fat inner thighs
Against the pale blue sky,
His scream tore the cloud to shreds
Against the pale blue Northern sky,
But she only smiled and continued to love him
Against the pale blue sky.
As dogs bayed, geese honked South
Against the pale blue Northern sky.

Florida Sunset: Feb 6, 1972

Come have a look.
At my icebear neverrear dreadnaught.
So as to back up stand off jump down
Turn around bale a pick of cotton.
And they're off at Hialeah.
Bandy flamingo standard orang-u-tan.
People with ice cream guzzled bellies,
Scars of decades of making it and proving it made
Left hanging in front of their hips.
Pendulous drama of imagination,
Swinging, pregnant with dollars,
Come down south so their girls and boys,
Finely grown now, though plainly disaffected,
Visit and will return to Ponce de Leon's fountain,
Oh my fathers, come back, be grown—ups again.
Do not go gentle into that good night.
Rage, rage against the dying of the light
At Hialeah.

Ending

Sleep me up a dream,
I tell my solo self.
Fill my cup to overflowering,
slip me in an ivory knife.

Standing between dawn and morning,
erecting his usual wall, he is
turning his shoulder so my face
meets his backbone, my arms his
elbowing arms
presenting his heels to my
exploring thighs, he
runs from me in his sleep.

Dorothy

She unwound her days like a ribbon.
She took crimson satin off her spool of pain,
She had good to give and she gave it.
She had good to take and she took it.
She unwound her days like a ribbon.
She took crimson satin off her spool of pain.
Walking down your spiral, you can't see where you're going, only
    somebody's trail,
She unwound her days like a ribbon.
She took crimson satin off her spool of pain.

Days

Days from Sault St. Marie
Too much oil in my hair,
Afraid he will discover I think in literary terms,
Words, the pith of which is one one's darling joy.
Yes, thus, slender, chic, yes
on slag piles
shot-up words on heaps of bodies
Wasted on a hill in Vietnam
Hanging flags between corpses
I love the American ineptitude for lies
Which ensures the CIA getting caught
Always the same kind of history-mangling that
Everyone's done forever
Pace.

Countercongruity

People on subways
Poetry on index cards
Sex in clinics,
Compulsively.
Turning the irregular patterns, rough hospital sheetlike,
Into. Mitered square corners crossover here.
Whistle stop. Flight path.
X marks the spot where cognitive skills coalesce into the
treasure map boundary substance come together.
Turn.
Subways powered by people
Index cards fill the posts, hands-on gifts to open- handed givers
Clinics deserted while we do it in the red carpeted royal green
Bower winding long road.

Chiaroscuro Dialogue

White: Swept by waves of nausea,
Undercome with fear and troubling,
Darkness, womanhood clarity.
Warning to move her taster and first
Isolated on a green and beige straw woven
Subway carseat
Speak roughly to your little boy and
Beat him when he sneezes
He only does it to annoy because
He knows it teases,
Black: Can she will she stay? Even if pushed?
Is she a summer soldier, On the Make?
A balloon, leftmensch, Ariel?
Cold, demanding, mean?
Crudely simple, soapily, mushily warm?
Turning to slime when dissolved in warm water?
Crushing, steel against brass-like
Hammered nails. Has she the hit with a chisel teeth
that could, if needed, hold on?
Grays:
This as thickness, ill beyond health
Certain only that we are lost in the mists.
All together, we hear our voices loudly reverberating
As in the darkest stalactite caves, echoing,
Augmented by those bounced off sound waves to
Enrich and magnify our Amen.

Bus trip

Seventy-year-old lady,
thin limbed in your silver crochet dress,
silver hat upgraced by tall fore-brim,
beige coat and shoes,
silvery transparent plastic umbrella,
you are the ultimate in chic.
Pancake makeup deepens hollows in your cheeks.
Earned spurs, souvenirs, medals, stamps
you paid for in full on the installment plan.
Now you cash in on all the torn-off days.

Amazing Grace

When I hear of those who go lusting after poetry
Wanting, like Frost, to be poets, to make a career of that
I wonder how it can be. Don't they feel that terror
of the demon muse, Inspiration?
That night terror, bringer of the blood sucker who
Draws reddening skin into serrated eclipse,
   digesting
It past, coagulating into baby food.
Is it that they don't see the danger stop sign?
Or do they face the monster willingly,
Glad to turn away from emptiness?
The pitcher empties before it can be replenished,
As the old Greek couple found. The more I write,
The more she bears me gifts and comes.
Despite my own intent, not Mercury-ankled
But woman she comes.
Fearful-breasted Athena Amazon.

Aaron

Not, I am not
and why should I be
his secretary
putting words to
his ideas

I am the older brother
Deserve respect
I speak in tones
Of beauty

I splash words
Skipping them
like stones
across the waves
of the red sea

Their heads life to hear me
I will not hammer
Sharp words on
Resisting stone

Too tedious for me
I am and say
And this is
Enough for people
For ever

1880

True repentance averts the evil decree
Shattering bone leaves peppery shards of fear
To comb reality's hair with,
Bring tears from clogged ducts' eyes
Pull down the shofar snake.
Clearly, as they say: clear, as it is said,
With light and water, air and fire,
You unify the sand boundary.
Used it to be subway pulse short ago in Kansas
That I missed so much, so much I was empty all
around it? With the missing thing's place
The center of a huge spiraling wind, roaring
Emptiness across the Great Plains like a tornada?
The saltiest tears pass through kidneys after you have sucked
Them back from your eyes.
Bitterest hate come from the heart regurgitating love's
      Unloving:
Sourest rancor is breast-milk's whey evaporated.
And sweetness, one self is born in the dungy.

Beware

Wary now, I can't tell when they will spring.
The bogey-man of my pleading unpunished because
Uncommitted sins. The simpletons who
have already have them and been beaten.
Whipped hard enough to make the blood stand in beads, like sweat,
with chains, bats, balls spiked, handled in iron.
      steel grey motions.
"If you don't behave, I'm going to throw you in the garbage can."
She told her four-year-old summer daycare victim.
And she did. Screaming pushed him,
Sweating showed him. Out.

Tante Marianne: The Spinster

I am a scavenger of cousins.
I gather them up in buzzing swarms
At sizzling bar—mitzvahs In the suburbs.
Circling with black silk quilted sleeves,
Pressing them to pale never
      uncovered in sunlight.
Pendant breasts. I suck them up to my
      blood red nipples.
Hoping they can relieve the press of milk
      to feed children I never bore.

Three Tempos 4:4:3

Monster baby/wrap your fingers around my pole.
It's the be all/do all/end all/American horse-gaited
quarter horse/syncopated rage/monster baby.
That's all.

Slipping awayness/shading silk-like downtown
on a lateral sideshow. Two over one down.
Teach my smoothed down ignorance, my daughter.
Choose to acknowledge what needs to be changed.

Flop, zap, gonna deedledum baseball rap.
Tweed deedle, I'm three quarters over,
Waltzing along beside the abyss.

HAIKUS

Dawn November 20, 2019

Rosy East devolves:
yellow, green, white-clouded blue.
Black panther day strikes.

Sunrise Walk

Twenty-three minutes
to home shadows elongate west
I scare myself.

Stride, stride, stride, stride bump
stride, stride, stride bump stride stride bump
stride bump, stride bump, bump.

Crito

Socrates gave rise
to Plato but also to
Alcibiades.

Disappointment

Brilliant sweet cherry
red dawn horizon portends
hot black sea storm day.

Morning Love Song

Spiky green, velvet green,
leaves tear-shaped green open my
dawn-green eyes to you.

Koan for Cohen

Why did God create
the world? They love stories, sound,
colors, shapes, and tears.

March 24, 2020

Orion's diamond
belt pulls black velvet sky up
towards infinity.

March 24, 2020

Clouds darker than sky
virus panic covers us
loneliness shuts me.

April 15, 2020

Sun turns cloud palest
baby pink on ice-blue sky
I am reaching toward.

Walking into dawn.

Leftover crescent moon
slices into blue atmosphere:
burnt away by sun.
Billowing clouds hover
slate-grey underlining blue
pain, my latest friend.

Plague June 20, 2020

Lemon streak slices
Eastern dank bee horizon
now wait for the scorch.

2 a.m. in Wuhan

Sitting outside time
He texts New York from China
darkness into light

End of Story

And they lived to the
end of their days and they were
very happy sometimes.

Grey overshadows
Sunset clouds layered pink, blue
pink, green, pink, grey, blue.
Note to Georgia O'Keefe

Hibiscus opens
pink, deep, luscious bloom becomes
strong: vulva.

Aging

Bitter sunlight pales
roses fade, grass blades sharpen,
sun downs, roses glow.